IMAGES
of America

SALEM TOWNSHIP

This 1901 photograph shows the Benjamin Shuck family working in the fields. Neighbor Martin Palmbos is helping them out. The large field behind them with the straw gathered together in shocks shows they had been working at it for a while. This piece of equipment was called a grain binder and was pulled by three horses. Shown from left to right are (first row) Benjamin Shuck, Oria Shuck, Forest Shuck, and Palmbos; (second row) Guy Shuck. (Courtesy of Judi Montgomery.)

On the cover: Another long day of threshing for these Market Street men is pictured. Fall found them gathering at each other's farms to harvest their crops. These men were using a steam engine and a threshing machine. Each pitchfork is three pronged to help gather straw at harvesting. The farmers in this area grew wheat, barley, rye, and oats. (Courtesy of Roberta Becker.)

IMAGES
of America

SALEM TOWNSHIP

Dianna Berens Beaudoin, Jean Loedeman Lam, and Susan Kipen
Welton for the Salem Historical Committee

ARCADIA
PUBLISHING

Published by Arcadia Publishing
Charleston SC, Chicago IL, Portsmouth NH, San Francisco CA

Library of Congress Control Number: 2009933631

For all general information contact Arcadia Publishing at:
Telephone 843-853-2070
Fax 843-853-0044
E-mail sales@arcadiapublishing.com
For customer service and orders:
Toll-Free 1-888-313-2665

Visit us on the Internet at www.arcadiapublishing.com

This book is dedicated to the memories of our parents, Adam and Edna Kipen, Gerrit "Bob" and Fenna Loedeman, and Mary Bellinger. They have left us with a legacy of faith in God, love of family, and an appreciation of history. Many thanks to Roger Berens, who continues to share his passion for history.

CONTENTS

ACKNOWLEDGMENTS

We would like to thank the Salem Township community for sharing their family photographs and for answering our endless questions. There were many who allowed us to come into their homes and scan their precious family photographs. We wanted to assure those that with modern technology, we can share our wonderful past with others and their photographs would not be harmed. Once this was realized, many wanted to share.

Special thanks go to Elenora (Raab) Zischke, Edna (Curtis) Kipen, and Warren Smith. Zischke, who is 94 and still mows her lawn, shared with us her knowledge of the past of the Market Street area. Smith, who is 97 years young and still plows snow from his driveway, has shared with us his knowledge of the Burnips area. Kipen, who had shared wonderful stories of her life growing up in Salem Township, passed away in 2007 at age 94.

Thanks to Nan Schictel for sharing information concerning St. Mary's dedication and Kiemass. Special thanks to our husbands Craig Welton, Donald Lam, and Peter Beaudoin for encouraging and supporting our goal of publishing this book.

INTRODUCTION

Salem Township has been in existence for over 150 years. It was part of Monterey Township but then became a township of its own in October 1855. The majority of the early settlers were of German descent, a large portion of whom came through Ohio. The township was built by hardworking people who had a deep sense of faith in God.

The following pages show a brief personal glimpse into the past lives of the people of Salem Township and reflect the events that shaped the future generations.

Into the solitude of the mighty forest came the first white settler's sounds of horse's hooves and shouts of men seeking a new home to settle in. The quiet gave way as more and more settlers came into the area. They came from far to settle here since land was cheap and wood and game was plentiful. They could hear the howling of wolves under the starlight sky, and they hunkered over their campfires for warmth and safety. By day, they cleared enough trees to put up a shelter, and soon they had cleared enough land to plant their crops. The men that had come into the forests sent for their families since their shelters were ready. Every person in a family, no matter how young or old, was expected to help with the planting, harvesting, and chores to make everyday life possible.

They cleared the land and established sawmills to cut the woods into boards to build homes, churches, and businesses. The lumber was also sold to neighboring communities.

They brought their faith and met in each other's homes and soon built wooden structures in which to worship God. Soon many denominations sprang up throughout the township, and each family could worship in their own way.

As the need arose, businesses came into this small settlement and brought goods to meet the needs of the families. The small towns bustled, with farmers coming in for trading and supplies. Four small towns were established during this time: Burnips Corners, Diamond Springs, New Salem, and Salem Center. Before that time, the people traveled by foot or horse to the big towns of Allegan, Holland, or Grand Rapids. Some folks lived in the small communities and did not farm but instead ran various businesses. They kept their horses and chickens for eggs in their stables.

People in the community still talk about the great 1937 fire of the Burnips Hotel, during the worst electrical storm that many had ever witnessed. An earlier fire destroyed an original hotel on the site, and lightening then destroyed the second one. There were unique businessmen that come to mind, such as Joe Gorden, who as a furniture maker in the 1900s also sold coffins in his store. He heard about a new procedure called embalming, so he traveled to Grand Rapids to learn about this skill in a seminar. He then became the first undertaker in the area to embalm the deceased.

Burnips was the home of Hudsonville Ice Cream, the ice cream of choice for much of lower Michigan. This creamery moved to Burnips in 1948 and was a large part of the community until it moved to Holland in 2003.

Schools were established to educate the growing numbers of children. There were nine one -oom schools throughout the township, placed a certain distance from each other since the children walked to school. The walk to school was sometimes a fun-filled happy time with friends through fields and streams. During the winter months, they still walked to school in their woolens, and if they were lucky, they could catch a ride on a buckboard going by. The children carried their lunch pail with sandwiches made of lard spread over bread. During the cold weather, the children brought a potato and set it next to the wood stove to cook for lunch. Playing ball was a favorite pastime of the schoolchildren. They made up teams and played against neighboring schools to see which would be the champion. This allowed them to visit and make new friends in neighboring schools. The one-room schools only went up to the eighth grade. Any child wishing to continue onto high school traveled to the Burnips School, which only went to 10th grade.

Many young people met in groups and paired off. There were many buggies or Model Ts slowly making their way down the sandy trails in the country. Many marriages were decided under the stars. Permission needed to be granted by the parents before a marriage was announced.

The men of the community enjoyed hunting and fishing once chores were done. This brought friends together to reminisce and swap stories of the big one that had gotten away. Since game was still plentiful, this brought food to the table and sport for the men. The Depression saw many menfolk out hunting, fishing, or trapping to put food on the table in really hard times.

Women of the community cared for each other during and after childbirth or sickness. They worshipped together and held picnics and quilting bees. They worked right alongside the men harvesting, and then they canned or preserved the meat, fruit, and vegetables. They also sewed their own family's clothing, made their own soap, and presided over weekly baths. One tub full of water was used for the entire family, and one hoped to not be the last one.

Life was extremely difficult, but there was always time for a barn raising, ice-cream social, house party with dancing, horseshoes, and ballgames. The Independent Order of Odd Fellows, the Sons of Veterans, and the Rebekahs were among some of the societies in Salem Township.

Many a tear was shed to see a son or loved one march off to serve the country. Almost every family was affected. Those represented in the photographs in the following pages are just a small sampling of the many men who served. The people of Salem Township have a deep pride in each one of the men and women who have served no matter in what capacity.

In the 1930s, oil was discovered in the township, which brought in the "Oil People" from the outside. This era quickly changed a very quiet community into a rough and boisterous place. The oil found on a farm could sometimes mean the difference between losing the farm and keeping it. These were hard days. As the oilmen came, every available room was rented out to house them. There are still some of the oil families that call Salem their home.

By publishing this book of photographs, stories, and memories, part of the past has been preserved and a continuing sense of pride in the community has been instilled. The Salem Historical Committee motto is "Preserving Salem History for Future Generations". That is the intent with publishing this book.

The authors have sought to be as factual as possible. The memories and stories have come from a diverse group of people within the community. If the authors apologize if they have inadvertently misidentified a person or misrepresented a memory.

One

FACES OF YESTERDAY

The matriarch of this five-generation photograph is Catherine (Strickfaden) Drier (sitting), Shown from left to right are her daughter Rosina Paffhouse Sebright, her granddaughter Katherine Homrich, her great-granddaughter Eleanor McLanchan, and great-great-grandson Harold Faye Orcutt (in her lap). Catherine lived to be 93 years old and is buried in the Salem Township Cemetery. She came to Salem in the 1850s with her father, Charles. (Courtesy of Dorothy Paffhouse.)

The Stickley family poses here for a photographer. Adam Stickley's parents came to Salem about 1855 and purchased land in sections 18 and 19. He was born in 1853 in Ohio and died on May 30, 1891, in Salem Township. He married Mary Rummelt, daughter of Charles and Maria Schwander. To them were born five children, three of whom lived to adulthood. From left to right are Adam, Dora, William, Mary, and baby Philip (front). (Courtesy of Dianna Beaudoin.)

Adam and Louisa Esterly Raab pose with their family in this early 1900s photograph. They settled in Salem Township in 1855 on section eight. Adam's son John claimed the distinction of being the first child born in Salem. Shown from left to right are (first row) Adam, John, Charles, Christina, and Louise; (second row) Isabel, Henry, Catherine, Matilda, Sarah, and Louisa. (Courtesy of Lorne and Vivian Buhler.)

This photograph is of the John and Catherine (Stickley) Claus family. Shown from left to right are (first row) John and George; (second row) son John and Catherine. John and Catherine were married on May 19, 1867, in Salem Township by J. Schladenaude, the pastor of St. Paul's Lutheran Church. They lived on section 19 and later moved to section 16. (Courtesy of Dianna Beaudoin.)

This photograph is of the John and Catherine (Strickfaden) Drier family. Shown from left to right are (first row) Ida, Catherine, John, and Charles; (second row) Margaret, Joseph, Caroline, John, Rose, William, Wilhemina, and Sophia. John and Catherine were married in her father's home in 1861 in Salem Township and lived across the road from him on section eight. (Courtesy of Dianna Beaudoin.)

This is a formal portrait of the Gerrit and Gertie Brower family. Their farm was located on Thirty-fourth Street in the early 1900s. Although they lived on Thirty-fourth Street, all their children were born in Drenthe. Gertie passed away in 1925. Shown from left to right are (first row) Ann, mother Gertie, father Gerrit, Helen, and Ralph; (second row) Harry, Dick, Nick, Herm, Tony, and Ben. (Courtesy of Lyle and Betty Brower.)

The George and Loretta (Green) Smith family pose for this family photograph. Shown from left to right are (first row) George, with grandson Ralph Cole (Leila's son) on his lap, and Loretta; (second row) Lela, George "Elmer," and Frank. George's father, Elial, and his mother, Catherine, came to Salem Township in 1854 from Findley, Ohio, and settled on section 15. When George's parents died, he took over the farm, and his family still resides on this land in 2009. (Courtesy of Dene and Colleen Smith.)

Annie Smith sits spinning yarn out of sheep's wool. She lived on this farm for more than 75 years. She was born in Austria in 1869 and came to America on a ship with her mother and three older siblings when she was eight. Her father had preceded the family by six months to establish their home. She met her future husband, Frank J. Smith, on the ship and married him when she was 15 years old. (Courtesy of Margaret Weber and Marian Streb-Albers.)

Charles Strickfaden was born October 4, 1820, in Germany to Michael and Cresentia (Bechler) Strickfaden. At age 11 in 1832, he came to the United States with his father. Charles married Margaretha Goodman on January 6, 1841, in Ohio and came to Salem in 1853. Their family consisted of 14 children, 12 whom lived to adulthood. Charles died on February 12, 1904, and rests in St. Mary's Cemetery. (Courtesy of Dianna Beaudoin.)

Christian and Mary Sutter were married on May 5, 1853, in Buffalo. They came to Salem Township in September 1856 and settled on section two. To them, four children were born: Charles, Adam, Christian Jr., and Frederick. Christian served in the Civil War and held several offices in Salem. He and Mary are both buried in the old section of the Salem Cemetery. (Courtesy of Art Oldenbeck.)

Elias and Sarah (Moored) Shuck came to Salem Township sometime between 1864 and 1865 from Marian Township, Hancock County, Ohio. They settled in the northern part of the township in section three and had nine children: Amanda, William, Benjamin, Elizabeth, Julia, John, George, Floretta, and Alexander. Elias was with the 9th Michigan Infantry, Company I, Allegan County. He was mustered out on June 20, 1865. (Courtesy of Judi Montgomery.)

Brothers Herman (seated) and Daniel (left) Brenner along with an unidentified friend are shown posing with cigars in their mouths. Herman was a conductor for the interurban train out of Grand Rapids. Herman's and Daniel's parents, Daniel and Julia (Raab) Brenner, were farmers. Daniel Sr.'s parents immigrated to the United States in 1862 with their three children, Samuel, Gottlieb and Daniel, and settled in Salem shortly after. (Courtesy of Dorothy Paffhouse.)

Jacob and Christina (Miller) Fleser settled in section five. All 11 of their children were born in this home. They later bought a home on section eight. Shown from left to right are (first row) Jacob Jr., Katherine, Christina, Jacob, Frederick, and William; (second row) Lucille, Elizabeth, Emma, Bertha, and Fredericka (died as a teenager). Jacob and Christina are both buried in the Salem Township Cemetery. (Courtesy of Brent Moomey.)

Jacob and Elizabeth (Esterly) Raab came to Salem Township in 1854 from Ohio and had 12 children. He returned to Germany at least once to bring his mother and brother Adam to America. In 1868, Jacob gave one acre of land for the building of a church. The Raabs lived on section eight and both Jacob and Elizabeth are buried in the Salem Township Cemetery. (Courtesy of Dorothy Paffhouse.)

James and Sarah (Mauch) Dibble owned a general store in Burnips Corners from 1879 to 1886. Dibbles sold dry goods, groceries, drugs, notions, boots, and shoes. The store was destroyed by fire in 1886. Shown here are James, his wife, Sarah, and their two children, Henry and Ida. (Courtesy of Stan Navis.)

John and Elizabeth (Schlegel) Strickfaden were married in the home of her father, Balthasar Schlegel, on December 6, 1862. To them, seven children were born of which six lived to adulthood. Shown from left to right are (first row) Laura, Elizabeth, John, and Dora; (second row) Mary, Christina, Lavina, and Joseph. They settled on section nine and later moved to section five. John held the office of constable for Salem for three years. (Courtesy of Loren Berens.)

This photograph shows Balthasor and Genovefa Schlegel's children. Balthasor was one of the early settlers in Salem. Shown from left to right are (first row) Catherine, who married Philip Fleser; Christine, who married Francis Goodman; Joseph, who married Catherine Goodman and later Caroline Miller; and Mary Ann, who married William Goodman; (second row) Caroline, who married Thomas Hinton; John, who married Susanna Lovina Smith; and Elizabeth, who married John Strickfaden. (Courtesy of Loren Berens.)

Mathias Kleibush was born in 1842 in Wirges, West Germany. He served in the military under the kaiser. The soldiers fare was so poor that he deserted and came to America and settled in the North Dorr vicinity. He married Mary Steffes in 1871 and had 10 children. (Courtesy of Dorothy Kroll.)

This 1921 photograph shows siblings Lawrence and Gertrude Green, children of Lawrence Green Sr. Clem and Freda (Smith) Green are shown standing in front of their home on 144th Avenue. Notice the lack of shoes and the well-patched pants. This was a family of hardworking farmers, like many others that lived in Salem Township on section nine. (Courtesy of Warren Smith.)

Peter and Anna Maria "Emma" (Schneider) Kipen are pictured here with their children shortly before she passed away. From left to right are (first row) Adam, Elizabeth, Emma, and Lawrence; (second row) Emma, holding Oliva, and Peter, holding Clara. The mother, Emma, passed away on February 19, 1917, leaving her very young family with their father. Peter kept the children together, and the two older girls stepped in to take care of the family, a big responsibility. (Courtesy of Susan Welton.)

Aunts and uncles were sometimes born just years apart from their nephews and nieces, as this photograph depicts. From left to right are Vern Willyard, Francis Curtis, and Jeanette Willyard. Standing in front is Clyde Curtis. Maurice Curtis is standing on the chair, and Viola Curtis is holding her baby sister Edna Curtis, who was born in 1913. (Courtesy of Susan Welton.)

There was always a table full of good food when the Kipen family got together for Sunday dinner. The women of the family all brought a dish or two to share for the family to enjoy. Shown from left to right are (first row) Betty Zerfas, Emma Winchester, Clara Kitchell, and Oliva Kipen; (second row) Edna Curtis Kipen, Emmaline Thomas Kipen, and aunt Katie Schneider Dusendang. (Courtesy of Susan Welton.)

Sunday family dinners were always great fun. Parents talked and laughed while the cousins all played together, having a ton of fun. These children are the Zerfas, Kipens, and Leonards. Shown from left to right are (middle) Francis (Genie), Adam R., Richard, Robert, Jean, Theresa, Evelyn, Dolores, Marilyn, Doris, and Phil; (rear) Orville, Norman, Gerald, Orell, Arline, and Janet. Families lived close, and time marched on at a slower pace. (Courtesy of Susan Welton.)

20

The William A. and Sarah (Willyard) Curtis family is shown. From left to right are (first row) Lauren, mother Sarah holding Lavonna, father William A., Clara, Homer, and Lena in front of her father; (second row) Maurice, Edna, Francis, Clyde, and Viola. William taught at many schools in the area, including Burnips, Diamond Springs, Overisel, Monterey, Pickle Street, and Dallas . Sarah hired out, caring for expectant mothers during and in the weeks following childbirth. (Courtesy of Susan Welton.)

This early-1900s photograph is of Christian Loew. Christian and Mary Loew came to Salem Township in 1865 along with his brother Frederick. They settled on section eight and had 12 children. Two of their sons, Daniel and Martin, also became farmers in Salem. Christian was born on June 14, 1825, in Wurtemburg, Germany, and died on November 25, 1912. He and Mary are both buried in Salem Township Cemetery. (Courtesy of Don and Janice Loew.)

It was a rare occurrence to have a family's photograph taken. Jacob and Theresa (Schumacher) Weber sit with their children around 1912. The smile on Theresa's face shows the pride in her family. Shown from left to right are (first row) Theresa, Nellie (Gegoski), Ethel (Burger), Genieve (Baker), and Jacob holding Lucille (Higbee); (second row) John, Anna (Kipen Harnish), Theresa (Seewald), Matilda (Dusendang), and Frank. (Courtesy of the Miller family.)

Joseph Schumacher was born in 1830 in Maisborn, Rhineland. He came to America in 1846 with his family. He married Elizabeth Hye in 1854 and settled in Salem Township. They had four children by the time Elizabeth died. Later Joseph married Theresa Gerlich and fathered 12 more children. He raised his family on his 35-acre farm in New Salem. He died in 1909. (Courtesy of the Miller family.)

It was picture day for the Anton and Elizabeth Kelling Junglas family. Dressed up in their Sunday best, the family poses for the photographer. Shown from left to right are (first row) Anna, Elizabeth , baby Elizabeth, and Anton; (second row) Peter, Joseph, and William. The couple's five older children were no longer at home when this photograph was taken around 1884. (Courtesy of the Miller family.)

Jacob and Magdalena Kreiser Schumacher pose for the photographer with their six oldest children. Shown from left to right are (first row) Magdalena holding Clara, Jacob Jr., and Jacob holding Frances; (second row) Joseph, John P., and Theresa. The girls' lace collars appear to be handmade. This photograph may have been taken outside since there is grass on the ground. Jacob owned New Salem Saloon. (Courtesy of the Miller family.)

What a joyous event weddings are. This was John Schichtel and Theresa Schumacher's wedding day on August 2, 1910. They were married at St Mary's Catholic Church with their families in attendance. Shown from left to right are (first row) Elizabeth and John Schichtel, Jake and Magdalena Schumacher, Theresa Schumacher, and Catherine and John Schichtel Jr.; (second row) John Schichtel, Theresa Schumacher, Frances Schumacher, and Ed Schichtel. (Courtesy of the Miller family.)

Four young friends took time out to pose for the photographer around 1900. From left to right are (standing) Joseph Junglas; (seated) Jacob Heibel, William Junglas, and Joseph Kreiser. The background of the portrait is similar to other family photographs of that era. A photographer may have been in the area, possibly taking family pictures at a church. The straw and grass suggest it was taken outdoors (Courtesy of Miller family.)

The William Heasley family posed for this photograph in 1895. Shown from left to right are (first row) Mary Patterson, wife of a Dorr Township blacksmith; mother Isabella (Merchant) Heasley; (second row) William Jr., a dentist in Zeeland; Joseph, a doctor (ENT) in Grand Rapids; Aaron, a farmer on section five; Wilson Henry, a doctor in Burnips; Lewis, a teacher and farmer on section nine. (Courtesy of Gene and Donna Heasley.)

Grandpa John Raab sits while happily holding two of his grandchildren. The little boy and girl are dressed in their Sunday best to have their photograph taken with him. Raab's enormous hands are cradling his precious charges. The expression on his face says it all: he loves these grandchildren. The children are unidentified. (Courtesy of Roberta Becker.)

John Moored and his wife, Amanda, purchased 80 acres on section nine in 1854. It was not until 1857 that they came to Salem to live with their two children, Elias and William. They lived in a log house until a second home was built for them in 1880 by his brother Patterson Moored. John and Amanda had six more children, Dallas, James, Kelly, Ann, Wesley (Sherman), and Oliver. (Courtesy of Lyman and June Moored.)

Please provide a caption.

Adam Endres and his wife, Elizabeth, are standing in front of their home, which was a boardinghouse at the time of this photograph and was located next to St. Mary's Church. The woman and child in the horse and buggy are most likely family visiting. The Endres walked 22 miles from New Salem to Grand Rapids to be married. This photograph is from the 1890s. (Courtesy of Al Wycoff.)

Antonius Striegle was born on November 27, 1837, to Joannes and Theresia (Huschkau) Striegle. The family lived in Ketzelsdorf, Bohemia. Antonius married Theresia Stoelzel and had four children. They came to America in 1875 and settled near the New Salem area, where they had their last two children. (Courtesy of Shirley Hilaski and Kathleen Cornett.)

Carefree days of childhood on the farm quickly fly by. These little barefoot boys seem to be enjoying their day of playing hard. Young Albert and Frank Streigle have stopped playing long enough to have their photograph taken around 1907. They were two out of six children born to Wentzel and Catherine (Dusendang) Striegle. (Courtesy of Shirley Hilaski and Kathleen Cornett.)

New Salem resident Josefus Striegle and Alice Gass were married in October 1903. This photograph shows the young couple with their attendants. The bride's friends May and Rosa Darga served as her attendants. The groomsmen were Alice's brother Frank Gass and Josefus's brother Antony. (Courtesy of Shirley Hilaski and Kathleen Cornett.)

Two

LIVING OFF THE LAND

The Elmer Smith family is pictured during harvesting of their oat field, with their trusted team of horses Fred and Prince. Smith was almost finished when his children came out to see him. Oscar holds the reins, Clyde is the oldest (rear), Warren is to the right, Dolly is in front, and Arden plays with the dog. Daughter Etta took the photograph with her box camera. (Courtesy of Warren Smith.)

Cutting trees down by hand was a back-breaking job. Friends and neighbors Martin Palmbos and Guy Schuck are taking a break on the tree they had just cut down. They were using two different axes: one to cut the tree down and one to split the wood. They would next have to cut the trees into pieces small enough to transport home, most likely on a sleigh. (Courtesy of Salem Historical Committee.)

Washday was an all-day process. Fenna Loedeman filled the washer, loaded the clothes into the machine, and ran them through the wringer into the rinse water twice. Loedeman is photographed in the 1950s hanging her clothes on the line. Rain or shine, hot or cold, the clothes were hung up. Wet clothes sometimes froze stiff on the line on a cold day. Loedeman's children Ruth and Jean often danced with the frozen shirts and coveralls. (Courtesy of Jean Lam.)

Men are feeding newly harvested wheat into a threshing machine to separate the stalk from the grain. Traveling from farm to farm, father and son team Steven and Gerrit (on the tractor) Loedeman rented out their thresher and steam-driven tractor during busy harvest season. The date on the barn is 1876. This photograph was taken in the mid-1940s. (Courtesy of Jean Lam.)

Gerrit (left) and his father, Steven Loedeman, are enjoying some refreshments during a break from threshing in the 1940s. Several farms in the neighborhood worked together to get their grain harvested. The farm that was being harvested at noon always provided a big dinner, sometimes including muskrat or turtle. If someone was too slow in serving himself, he could go hungry. (Courtesy of Jean Lam.)

Adam Kipen was hot and dusty since he had been hard at work in the fields with his team King and Bennie. His wife, Edna, along with their four oldest children, Dick, Dolores, Genie, and Maryilyn, brought Kipen something cold to drink. Kipen farmed the same land that his grandparents Johan and Maria Katherine and parents, Peter and Anna Maria Kipen, had farmed. This photograph is from the 1930s. (Courtesy Susan Welton.)

There are some chores that are fun and some that are just plain smelly. This is the case on the Henry Weber farm. Fred Weber, at 19 years old, stands on the left, with his friend 16-year-old Joe Funk on the right. The horse-drawn manure spreader is full and ready to be taken to the fields. This photograph was taken on Wednesday, July 22, 1885. (Photograph by John Weber; courtesy of Dorothy Kroll and Allen Wycoff.)

This is Little Rabbit River before it was dredged. Neighbors Anton Funk, John Gaza, Joe Funk, Joe Weber, Fred Weber, John Weber, the Frank and Lea Funk boys, Fred Weist, Tony Ratnof, and Leo Lenhart are all listed on this picture in no particular order. Note the two young boys in the rear holding the rocks. (Courtesy of Dorothy Kroll and Allen Wycoff.)

Standing wiht pitchfork in hand, Fred Weber is ready to tackle his chores. He was born on Thursday, September 16, 1886, one son of Henry and Gertrude Alfen Weber. Fred married Veronica Kleibush, and the couple had eight children. He was a farmer who raised cows, pigs, and chickens, from which he sold eggs. He also was a water well digger who was well known in the area. (Courtesy of Dorothy Weber Kroll.)

This early-1900s photograph shows Norman Sebright (front), Lynn Moored (center), and unidentified (rear) with a tie on, and an unidentified child working on boiling the sap down. The pile of ashes in front of them indicates they had been at it for a while. Notice the smoke rising from the fire. This was located on Moored's father, Oliver's, farm. (Courtesy of Lynn and June Moored.)

The only two identified in this photograph are Sebright (left) and Lynn Moored, holding the reins of the horse. They are gathering maple sap and pouring it into barrels. They hauled the barrel full of sap to the fire in the woods, where they boiled it down. When it was a certain thickness, they brought the remainder in the house to finish boiling it down. They then placed it in jars to use. (Courtesy of Lyman and June Moored.)

This early-1900s photograph shows Lynn Moored tending his sheep. The Mooreds lived on a farm north of Burnips on Thirtieth Street. Lynn's father, Oliver, and his grandfather John were all farmers in Salem. The sheep were raised for their wool and were shorn a couple times a year. Most likely, the wool was sold and some was used for personal use to be made into cloth. (Courtesy of Lyman and June Moored.)

Anna (Richter) Smith is holding the reins of her two horses, while her two daughters Mary (right) and Rose (left) sit on the barn hill in the background. Smith learned the life of a farmer at a young age. She was forced to quit school and take her place on the farm as her father's helper because there were no boys in her family. (Courtesy of Margaret Weber and Marian Streb-Albers.)

Harry Weber stands outside his sugar shanty after a newly fallen snow in the 1940s. The poker stick in his hand was used to stoke the fire in the pit under the two large sap pans. The mound of ashes on the ground in front of him that came from the burned wood was used to cook the sap down into maple syrup. Weber's entire family helped with this yearly event. (Courtesy of Margaret Weber and Marian Streb-Albers.)

Once a year, the men of the community cut wood to heat the German Methodist Church (also known as the Market Street Church), which was located on Thirty-second Street. Pictured from left to right in the early 1900s are Billy Moomey, Frank Miller, Joe Strickfaden, Bill Miller, Gottlieb Miller, Tony Berens, Harley Miller, John Drier, Pearl Sebright, Sylvester Raab, Jacob Miller, Sam Raab, Jacob Fleser, Charles Raab, Bill Drier, and Wes Raab sitting on the stump. (Courtesy of Elenora Zischke.)

The steam engine and threshing apparatus pictured was owned by VanSlooten. He went from farm to farm, as the neighbors all helped harvest each others fields; it was a community effort. The grain went into storage buildings called granaries to be used as feed, sold, or kept as seed for the next year. The straw was piled into large stacks to be used as bedding for the animals. This photograph is from the 1880s. (Courtesy of Elenora Zischke.)

Standing behind this 1920s Fordson tractor is Samuel Brenner, one of three sons born to Daniel and Julia (Raab) Brenner. An all-around handyman, Samuel was an electrician, plumber, photographer, and carpenter, and with his brother, he built his uncle Elmer Brenner's home. Samuel was unmarried but became a second father to his niece Dorothy Brenner. (Courtesy of Dorothy Paffhouse.)

Lambert Schipper and his youngest son, Les, are riding the corn boat. It rode between two rows of corn, and the knife attached to each side cut the corn. The cut corn stalks were then caught by the two men. When they had an armful, they stacked them up in the cornfield to dry. It was a dusty and hard job. (Courtesy of Lyle and Betty Brower.)

As wheat or oats were being threshed, the straw was blown onto the v-shaped boards in the background. The boards provided an opening for pigs to burrow into the straw piles for shelter during the winter. The grain was sold or stored for next year's crops. This is the farm of Lambert Schipper. It was located on Thirty-fifth Street in Salem Township. (Courtesy of Lyle and Betty Brower.)

This photograph of the Lambert and Dena Schipper farm shows the horses harnessed and ready to work. The leather straps hanging around them are to chase away the flies. The horses are standing idle, waiting to go into the fields to cut hay. Granddaughter Darlene Brower and her cousins are posing on the hay mower. This photograph was taken about 1950. (Courtesy of Lyle and Betty Brower.)

This is the Fred Sutter farm on butchering day. This hog weighed in over 500 pounds. The old saying goes, "They used almost all the pig except the oink." The head was boiled and used in head cheese, the fat was rendered into lard, the skin was fried into crackling, and the feet were made into pickled pig's feet. (Courtesy of Art Oldenbeck.)

William Strickfaden had help with this slaughtering day. Family and friends came together for this event, and every hand was needed. Six freshly slaughtered pigs hang on this temporary hanging frame. The men did the butchering and brought huge pans of meat into the house for the women to cut and preserve it. (Courtesy of Dianna Beaudoin.)

Raymond Weber stands in front of his bumper crop of wheat to show just how high it had grown in the 1940s. He farmed and grew different crops. Like all other families in the area, he had a large vegetable garden, and his potatoes grew right up to his wheat field. Weber also worked at a factory to help support his family. (Courtesy of Dorothy Kroll.)

William A. and Sarah "Sadie" (Willyard) Curtis are coming in from planting the spring garden. This garden was more than recreational during those times. It was hard work putting food on the table, including plowing the ground, raking it flat, laying the string for straight rows, and finally bending over or crawling along the ground to plant a long row of seeds while praying for a good harvest. (Courtesy of Susan Welton.)

Sisters Bertha (left) and Emma Fleser are standing in their father, Jacob Fleser's, pasture while holding on to the family horses around 1900. They lived on section nine on the corner of Thirty-second Street and 144th Avenue. Bertha married William Moomey, and Emma never married. (Courtesy of Lorne Berens.)

The four oldest children of Adam and Edna (Curtis) Kipen had great fun living on the farm. Shown here with the family goats, from left to right, are Dickie, Dolores, Eugene (Genie), and Marilyn. The farm was mostly all blow sand. The chicken coop is shown in the background. The chickens were used for eggs and an occasional chicken dinner. This family lived on 142nd Avenue. (Courtesy of Susan Welton.)

Melvin Berens and his younger brother Earl are holding their father, Tony Berens's, workhorses June and Prince. Melvin and his wife, Madeline, went on to have their own farm in Salem Township on 146th Avenue for over 50 years, milking Holstein cows. Upon Melvin's death, the farm was passed on to his son Boyd, who continued the tradition. (Courtesy of Lorne Berens.)

Jenny Smith, wife of Frank Smith, watches the maple sap boil down into maple syrup in the 1920s. The sap was gathered daily. It was boiled in an open pan in the grove of maple trees. A canvas tent protected the boiling contents from the elements. Later a wood framed, tin-roofed sugar shanty was built to house an evaporator. (Courtesy of Margaret Weber and Marian Streb-Albers.)

Jacob Hildebrand is working in the fields on his farm. Many hours were spent behind the drag with his team of horses. He lived on 142nd Avenue near Maplegrove School. Hildebrand and his wife, Beth, farmed the land for many years. Beth also taught at several of the one-room schools in Salem. (Courtesy of Roberta Becker.)

Forever etched in the memories of Salem Township neighbors is the sound of the steam engine that belonged to Gerrit "Bob" Loedeman. It was used in a threshing business and then inherited from his father, Steve Loedeman. The steam engine was fired up by Bob and driven around the neighborhood every holiday. Posing for the picture is Bob's wife, Fenna, standing in the steam engine cab. (Courtesy of Jean Lam.)

This June 5, 1922, photograph shows George Weber in the process of working his fields behind his trusted workhorses. This was his first cutting of hay for the year. After the hay was cut, it was gathered up with a rake and piled on a wagon to haul to the barn. Weber and his family lived on a farm on 146th Avenue in Salem. (Courtesy of Vicki Switzer.)

44

Farm work never seems to be finished. Bert Deters is shown sitting on a two-horse-drawn cultivator about 1900. He was cultivating a field on his farm near Thirty-fourth Street and 140th Avenue. His farm bordered Rabbit River. Deters was born on September 2, 1876, and married Fannie Lenters. They had 13 children. (Courtesy of Crystal Deters.)

On the farm, everyone pitched. Bert and Fannie Deters's farm was no different. Mrs. Bert Deters sits on a milking stool, while Fannie (left) is also milking a cow. Her daughter Grace is standing in the dark dress. Another daughter Lillian is seated, milking another cow. The lady with the light-colored dress holding a pail is unidentified. Bert is standing in the back. This photograph was taken around 1900. (Courtesy of Crystal Deters.)

Corn that is knee high by the Fourth of July usually means a good harvest in the fall. The young man in control of the three-horse team is Howard Loew. Wesley Loew, his father, is standing behind the corn cutter with a pail. They were working on Wesley's farm north of what is now the Fred Loew farm on 146th Avenue. (Courtesy of Crystal Deters.)

This is slaughtering day at Benjamin and Margaret (Gordon) Shuck's home. They had a big job ahead of them to dress out 11 hogs. Family and neighbors all gathered to help. It was usually an all-day event to process the meat for the winter food supply. The only people identified in this photograph are Benjamin and Margaret (far left). (Courtesy of Judi Montgomery.)

Benjamin Shuck is standing in the middle of his newly harvested wheat field. His home far in the background shows how much work they had to do to harvest this field. The photograph is looking southwest. It was the most eastern portion of Shuck's 160 acres. (Courtesy of Judi Montgomery.)

Here is another photograph of the Shuck farm. This view is looking northeast in section three. Notice Benjamin, with his hands tucked in his suspenders, giving direction. The grain binder shown cut the wheat and gathered it into small bundles. Neighbor Martin Palmbos is to the far left with his hands full, and his son Guy is standing next to the pile of wheat shocks. The shocks were gathered and brought up to the barn to be thrashed to remove the grain from the straw. (Courtesy of Judi Montgomery.)

It is ice harvesting time for the Benjamin Shuck family. The men gathered to cut the ice out of the pond in large blocks and haul it home in their wagons to store in the icehouse. The icehouse was insulated with sawdust to keep the ice from melting. The ice kept until it got too warm. The only person identified is Benjamin in the long overcoat. (Courtesy of Judi Montgomery.)

Wentzel Striegle went to church at St Mary's one Sunday morning in about 1925 and came home to do chores. He was surprised when Betty Meike was there snapping this photograph of him. Wentzel came to America as a child, on the ship the *City of Brussels*, on September 6, 1875, along with his parents, Antonius and Theresia (Stoezel) Striegle, and three siblings. (Courtesy of Shirley Striegle.)

Three

HEARTH OF THE HOME

Cyrus, his wife, Katherine (Schneider) Dusendang, and their son Raymond are standing in front of their clapboard-sided house. Their farm was just west of Burnips on 142nd Avenue. Notice the chimney is held up only by a wooden support, and the washer and washtubs are alongside of the house. Katherine had flowers in washtubs by the door to make the yard look pretty. Their home was very small and quaint. (Courtesy of Susan Welton.)

Here the Charles Wesley Loew family poses in front of their home. Seated in the chair to the left is Charles, his wife, Mary, is seated in the rear, daughter Sylvia is standing, and sons Virgil and Howard are shown with bib overalls on. The other two people are not identified. In 1923, a new home was built, and this one was torn down. (Courtesy of Gene and Donna Heasley.)

This is the Charles Wesley and Mary Loew farm. Charles rented this farm in the late 1800s, and in later years, he purchased it. They raised six children of which five grew to adulthood. Charles farmed this land, and many improvements were made over the years. He had milking cows, sheep, pigs, and chickens and raised wheat, corn, hay, and oats. This farm is still in the same family in 2009. (Courtesy of Gale Loew.)

50

This hip roof barn was built for Charles Wesley Loew. It was a common type of barn in this area. It was built in the late 1800s by timbers from Salem Township and torn down in the fall of 2004 by Charles's grandson Wendall and great-grandson Dan, who dismantled and rebuilt it on another location east of the current house on the same property. (Courtesy of Elenora Zischke.)

Three of the Loew men are identified in this 1911 photograph of their farm. They are standing out front among the cattle and horses. Shown from left to right are Charles Wesley Loew, son Virgil, son Howard, and unidentified. The silo on the left was in the process of being built. The other silo had been built in 1909. The largest barn was for milking cows. (Courtesy of Gene and Donna Heasley.)

This home was built for Cornelius and Helena DeJongh in the summer of 1907. Notice the carpenters with their tools on the porch and Cornelius standing at the top of the steps. The DeJonghs ran the general store next door from 1897 into the 1940s. They lived in this home until 1930s, when Herbert and Elenor Klinesteker bought it and turned it into a funeral home, which Herbert ran until the 1940s. (Courtesy of Elenora Zischke.)

Jacob and Dora Brenner came from Germany in 1859 with their four sons, Herman, Dan, Samuel, and Walter. They originally settled on Thirty-second Street on section nine and later moved to section five where this farm is located. Dan and his wife, Julie, took over running this farm. Dan's son Herman and his wife took over, and in later years, Herman's son Elmer ran it until he stopped farming in 1986. (Courtesy of Dorothy Paffhouse.)

This 1912 photograph is of Gotlieb and Margaret (Drier) Hildebrand's barn after a windstorm took it down. Family, friends, and neighbors all came over to access the damage. They were able to salvage the lumber and rebuild the barn. Gotlieb is the gentleman holding his hat in the middle of the photograph. The Hildebrands lived on 142nd Avenue near Thirty-fourth Street. (Courtesy of Roberta Becker.)

This photograph shows the home of John and Amanda (Rehinhammer) Moored. John purchased 80 acres in Salem in 1854 on section nine. He came to Salem to live in 1857 with his wife and two children. They lived in a log house until this home was built in 1880 by his brother Patterson Moored. This house is still standing in 2009 and is located on Thirtieth Street. (Courtesy of Lyman and June Moored.)

This home originally stood on Thirtieth Street. In 1881, it was moved to 146th Avenue to its present location with horses and tackle by Martinus and Grietje (Tiesinga) Palmbos. In 1900, their son Martin and his wife, Edith, who are pictured in this photograph, along with two of their children, purchased this home and resided there until 1945, when their son Lawrence and his wife, Lulu, took over the farm. In 1974, Lawrence's son Mark and his wife, Janice, purchased it and still reside there in 2009. (Courtesy of Bruce Palmbos.)

This home was owned by William (Bill) and Bertha Moomey from the 1920s to the 1950s. They were married on December 1, 1894, and had five children, Jacob, Newman, Arthur, Lloyd, and William. William died in 1950. This home is located on Thirty-second Street and is now owned by Merle and Phylis Immik. (Courtesy of Brent Moomey.)

Joannis and Maria Katherine (Rieser) Keupen built their home after they came to America in 1869. It started as a one-room home with a loft and was later added on to. They moved their one-story home by horse and logs from the back of their property to where it sits now on 142nd Avenue. A story and a half was added later by Joannis and his son Petrus, probably in a house-raising party. The two-by-fours for framing are one continuous board running from the peak to the basement. The boards used for the basement cement forms were reused as the sheathing on the upstairs inside walls. There are hand-hewn beams with bark on in the basement. The white slate siding and enclosed front porch was added, possibly in late 1950s. There have been four generations of Kipen's (or Keupen's) that have owned this home, including Peter and Emma Kipen, Adam and Edna Kipen, William Kipen, and currently Elizabeth (Kipen) and Cal Schaeffer. (Courtesy of Susan Welton.)

The David and Theda Jane Goodman family are shown in front of their home on Thirty-second Street. Shildren Honor and Faith are sitting in the buggy holding their trusted dog, while their father, David, mother, Theda Jane, and grandmother Harriet Walker are looking on. This home was destroyed by a tornado in 1965. (Courtesy of Roberta Becker.)

This Hildebrand family is shown in their cabbage patch near harvest time. Grandpa David Hildebrand is sitting on a stool in the patch with his family surrounding him. His son Gottlieb is on the far left, holding a dog in one arm and reins in the other hand. The man next to him is not identified. Gottlieb's wife, Margaret, is holding baby Fred, with Katie and John standing next to her. (Courtesy of Roberta Becker.)

Frederick and Bertha Sebright are seated in a buggy in front of their home on Thirtieth Street just south of Burnips. Bertha is holding their son Ferdinand, who was named after his uncle. Uncle Ferdinand had served in the Spanish-American War and the Civil War. The leather straps hanging down from the horses are to keep flies away. (Courtesy of Brent Moomey.)

William and Anna (Paffhausen) Strickfaden stand in front of their home on 144th Avenue. From left to right, the children are John, George, Elizabeth, little Christian, and Anna Mary. Mother Anna is expecting Sophia, and William's father Charles is shown in the center. Charles was one of the first settlers in Salem in 1853. This house still stands in 2009. The photograph was taken around 1891. (Courtesy of Dianna Beaudoin.)

Elmer and Elizabeth (Strickfaden) Smith and family are shown in front of their home on 143rd Avenue. Elmer's father, George, built this home, and it is still standing in 2009. Shown from left to right are Etta, Clyde, Dolly, and baby Warren sitting on his mother's lap. Elmer is standing in the rear. Warren remembers snow drifting across the floor when they woke in the morning. The photograph was taken about 1913. (Courtesy of Warren Smith.)

George and Loretta (Green) Smith are sitting on the front porch of their home. Their grandson Clyde, with his long curly hair, is sitting near them. Clyde's father, Elmer, is holding the reins of workhorses Fred and Prince, who were all harnessed and waiting to go into the fields. Their farm was located on 143rd Avenue. The photograph was taken around 1911. (Courtesy of Warren Smith.)

58

Joseph and Elizabeth (Fleser) Strickfaden stand in their yard with their children. From left to right are Emily on the horse, Joseph, Hazel, Fredericka, Elizabeth holding Katherine, Berth, and Pearl. The barn behind them was built by Joseph's grandfather Balthasor Schlegel in 1857. Joseph and Elizabeth worked this farm for many years. In 2007, this became a sesquicentennial farm owned by Balthasors great-great-grandson Boyd Berens. (Courtesy of Lorne Berens.)

This late-1800s photograph is of John and Katherine Strickfaden's home. Their four youngest children are standing by them: Caroline, Charles, Wilhemina, and Ida. They owned 80 acres on section eight near the sink hole on 144th Avenue. Katherine's father, Charles, was one of the first settlers in Salem. She and John were married on February 26, 1861, in Charles's home and had 12 children. (Courtesy of Roberta Becker.)

This early-1900s photograph shows an unidentified family sitting in the front yard of their home, which was located on the corner of Thirtieth and Newell Streets in Burnips. The Francis Moored family lived in this home for many years. It is still in existence in 2009 and is owned by Sheila Buckleitner. (Courtesy of Sheila Buckleitner.)

Barn raising parties were a common activity. John Dekleins barn raising was in 1908. Family, friends, and neighbors are all lined up on the barn. Local barn builder Charles Raab may have been their builder. The Dekleins lived on 146th Avenue between Thirtieth and Thirty-second Streets. This barn still stands in 2009 and is owned by Roger Berens. (Courtesy of Dianna Beaudoin.)

This is the home of Frederick and Isabelle (Raab) Bachman. A sign on the barn states "1908," when the barn was built. Isabelle, better known in the community as "Bell," is standing in the front yard. She and Frederick were married on October 5, 1893, in Salem Township. Frederick's parents, Christian and Mary Bachman, owned this land before he did. Frederick ran this farm until 1941, when it was sold to Melvin Berens. (Courtesy of Crystal Deters.)

This early-1900s photograph shows the home of Benjamin and Margaret Schuck. Benjamin's father, Elias Schuck, came to Salem in 1863 and purchased 131 acres in section three. In the late 1800s, Benjamin acquired this land from his father. The land has been home to several generations of Schucks and is still in the family in 2009. It is located on Loew Road. (Courtesy of Judi Montgomery.)

This home was built by Arthur DeJongh and his wife in the early 1900s, shortly after he moved to Salem Township. This 1914 photograph shows Arthur's wife, Carrie, their daughter Gladys, and their son Arthur sitting on the porch, while Arthur Sr. is in their car. It must have been cleaning day, as the rugs and pillows are strewn about the porch. Arthur Sr. and his brother Cornelius were merchants in Burnips. (Courtesy of Arthur and Carol DeJongh.)

Four

CHURCH BELLS RINGING

The German Methodist Episcopal Church was built in 1907 on Thirty-second Street. Local folks called it the Market Street Methodist Church. Jacob Raab had given an acre of land for the building of Zion Church in 1868. The church stood on this acre until 1906, when it was torn down and the German Methodist Episcopal Church was built. (Courtesy of Art Oldenbeck.)

In this 1907 photograph, the men from the German Methodist Episcopal Church are all holding up money from a fund-raiser to support building this parish. Charles Raab and Francis Buege were the builders. The man in the rear is Sylvestor Raab. Others identified from left to right include Martin Loew (second), Wesley Raab (fourth), and Fred Bachman (ninth). (Courtesy of Elenor Zischke.)

The Market Street Methodist Church Ladies Aid Society met at Charles and Mary Raab's house for this photograph. Shown from left to right are (seated) unidentified; (first row) three unidentified and Mary Loew; (second row) Freda Baachman, Rose Heasley, and Lucilla Raab; (third row) MaryAnn Moomey, Emily Win, Christina Buege, Isabella Bachman, Laura Miller, Elizabeth Strickfaden, Laura Raab, Elizabeth Strickfaden, and Elizabeth Miller. (Courtesy of Elenora Zischke.)

The Market Street Methodist Church was on the same circuit as Monterery Center Church, Salem Indian Mission, and the Burnips Methodist Church. Rev. Alton H. Zischke pastored all four churches. Families represented in this 1941 photograph are the Berenss, Buehlers, Browers, Harmsens, Millers, Hildenbrands, Loews, Bueges, VanSlootens, Raabs, Newells, Rynbrandts, Sebrights, Flesers, Strickfadens, Smiths, and Bachmans. (Courtesy of Elenora Zischke.)

The early beginnings of the German Methodist Episcopal Church, first known as the Zion Church and later known as the Market Street Methodist Church, started in the home of Casper Raab. It was later held in the homes of his nephews Jacob and Adam Raab and for one year was held in a schoolhouse. This church was built in 1868 on an acre of land that Jacob donated on Thirty-second Street. It was in existence until 1907, when this church was torn down and the new one was built. (Courtesy of Elenora Zischke.)

Grace Fleser, Carrie DeJongh, and Sherman and Mary Moored stand in front of the Burnips Methodist Church. The four were instrumental in leading many children to Christ through the grace of God. Sherman served as the Sunday school superintendent from 1901 to 1950, and his wife, Mary, also helped in various functions within the church. Fleser served as superintendent from 1950 to 1969. (Courtesy of Lyman and June Moored.)

Burnips Corners United Methodist Church was a brick building that was constructed in 1900 and used for 64 years. In 1964, the present church was built. Between 1945 and 1949, the members put a basement under this church at a cost of $4,000, which was loaned to the society by the Methodist Conference. The basement served as Sunday school classrooms. Rev. George Allen was the first pastor in this church. (Courtesy of Lyman and June Moored.)

This late-1940s photograph shows the congregation of Burnips Methodist Church standing in front of the church. Families represented in this photograph are the Mooreds, DeJonghs, Loews, Teeds, Newells, Ensings, Sheilds, Herps, Shucks, Parkers, Alwards, Coates, Penses, and Flesers. Rev. L. J. Washmuth, pictured second from left in back, was the pastor at the time. He served this church from 1945 to 1949. (Courtesy of Dene and Colleen Smith.)

Rev. Estey Batdorf was a lady preacher at the United Brethren Church in Salem, which stood on the corner of Thirtieth Street and 146th Avenue . Batdorf served in the late 1800s and was known to have aided in the conversion of many souls. This church was in existence until the late 1920s, when it was closed down. (Courtesy of Lyman and June Moored.)

In 1870, one acre of land was purchased from Charles Hoop on section nine for the intent to build a church for St. Paul's German Lutheran congregation. Early members of this church included the Alfens, Hoffmans, Millers, Hildebrands, Sutters, Flesers, Clauses, Slagels, Hoops, Raabs, Brenners, and Stickleys. This church was disbanded in 1927 and torn down in the 1930s. It was located near the Salem Township Cemetery. (Courtesy of Shirley Schepers.)

In 1873, this building was constructed for the congregation of the Church of God. It was located on Thirtieth Street across from the present-day United Methodist Church. In 1906, Silas Loew bought this building and moved it to the corner of Thirtieth Street and 143rd Avenue. He made berry crates in the basement and sold buggies and wagons from the upstairs. During the oil boom, it was converted to an apartment. This building is still in existence in 2009. (Courtesy of Lyman and June Moored.)

The dedication of St. Mary's Church in New Salem was held in June 1909. The pastor at that time was Fr. Reynold Kuehnel. His image is superimposed onto the church photograph above. From all accounts, his parishioners loved him, and there were 250 families in this parish. The photograph below shows the auxiliary bishop of Chicago leading the dedication service. There were over 500 people who attended this celebration. It was a warm, balmy day, and a dinner held in the church hall followed the service. The interior of the church was olive green with terra-cotta. There were hardwood floors that sloped so the altar could be seen from any part of the auditorium. Different families or groups donated money towards the purchase of many beautiful stained-glass windows. The gray exterior of the church was made from molded cement forms. (Courtesy of Allen Wycoff and the Miller family.)

Jesus! Maria! Joseph!

Zur frommen Erinnerung an

Franz Striegle,

geboren in Reinsdorf Oesterreich, am 7. Febru-
ar 1870; gestorben am Freitag, den 23.
August 1901, in New Salem Mich., Nach-
mittags um 2 Uhr, nach langem schweren
Leiden, wohlversehen mit den hl. Sterbe-
s-kramenten.

Ablaß Gebete.

Barmherziger Jesus, gib ihm die ewige Ruhe.
17 Jahre Ablaß.
Mein Jesus Barmherzigkeit. 300 Tage Ablaß.
Süßes Herz Mariä, sei meine Rettung. 300 Tage Ablaß.
Süßes Herz Jesu, gib daß ich immer mehr dich liebe.
300 Tage Ablaß.

Franz Streigle never married and died at the age of 31 of pneumonia in 1901. He was the son of Anton and Theresa Striegle. This holy card was given out at the time of his funeral. The Catholic Church gives out these cards in memory of loved ones. Streigle is buried at St. Mary's Cemetery. His family came to America in 1875 from Hungary. (Courtesy of Shirley Hilaski.)

Catholic parish life may have been strict, but it certainly was not joyless. The first known parish annual fund-raiser was a German kermis, after the term meaning "parish community fair," or bazaar. Money raised through kermis appears to have been used for building upkeep. Shown is the parish attending the fund-raiser, which was usually held outdoors. This photograph was taken about 1905. (Courtesy of the Miller family.)

70

This photograph was taken on the front steps of St. Mary's Church in New Salem on October 22, 1924. The bride is Rose Smith, and the groom is Harry Weber. Smith lived on a farm in Salem Township with her parents, Frank J. and Anna M. Smith. Weber lived on a farm in Monterery Center with his parents, Frederick and Katherine Weber. (Courtesy of Margaret Weber and Marian Streb-Albers.)

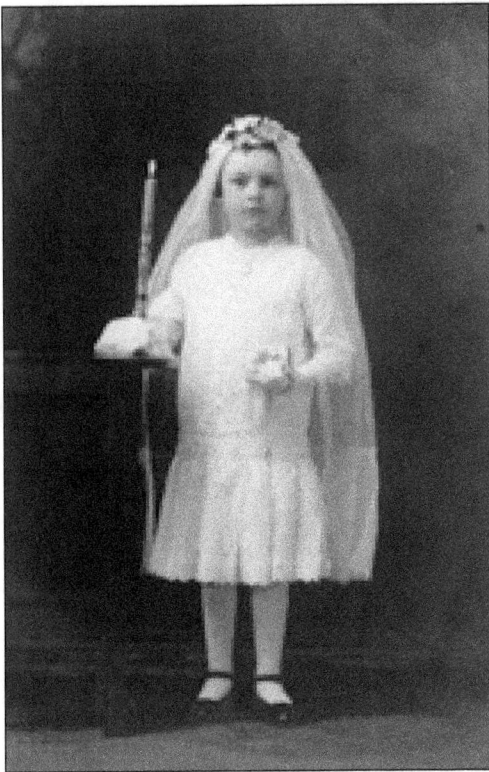

Agnes Junglas Miller, daughter of Peter and Elizabeth Schumacher Junglas, made her first communion in 1914. Agnes was raised as an only child, since her only sibling, Lucy Loretta, lived just two weeks in 1908. Agnes attended St. Mary's School for grades one through eight. Agnes and her husband John Miller became sole owners of New Salem Miller and Brooks Grocery between 1944 and 1964. (Courtesy of the Miller family.)

Here is Sylvester "Jack" Striegle on the day he received his first communion about 1919. He was among a group of children at St. Mary's that celebrated. It was customary for the little boys to wear suits and little girls to wear white dresses with veils. Here Striegle holds his first communion prayer book, rosary, and a candle. He was the son of Wentzel and Catherine (Dusendang) Striegle. (Courtesy of Kathleen Cornett.)

Five

GOING TO TOWN

This general store was built in 1886 for F. Goodman and Company. Brothers Cornelius and Arthur DeJoung purchased it from them in December 1893. The DeJoung family ran it for many years, and in 1944, Cornelius's son Fred took over and ran it until 1969. Here Cornelius, Arthur, and an unidentified person are standing on the front steps. The house to the left was Cornelius's residence. (Courtesy of Arthur and Carol DeJongh.)

This store was originally owned by a Mr. See, the first merchant in Salem Township. In 1856, he sold to James Burnip, and Burnip kept it for three years until he sold it to his soon-to-be son-in-law J. S Warner. Warner ran it for several years until he sold it to Wells and James R. Dibble in 1879. Dibble ran it until it burned on January 1, 1886. This building was located on the east side of the road where DeJonghs store stood. (Courtesy of Mary Navis.)

Dibble is seen front and center measuring out flour to be sold to a customer in his store. Dibble owned this store from 1879 to 1886, when it was destroyed by fire. Most items were kept in barrels and jars to be broken down and sold in smaller quantities. The lady on the right was waiting for her cloth to be cut for possibly a new dress. (Courtesy of Mary Navis.)

The fire department was organized in the early 1940s by local businesses feeling the need to have a group of men dedicated to fighting fires. This photograph shows the Salem Township Fire Department in the early 1950s. Pictured from left to right are Casey Kamps, Keith Hype, Norman Buege, Bill Moomey, Freeman Judy, Marshall (Mart) Simmons (fire chief), Wilmer "Jigs" Howard, Lloyd "Moose" Moomey, Clare "Jim" Newell, Luther Hildebrand, and Glen "Chuck" Selby. (Courtesy of Roberta Becker.)

This photograph shows the Salem Fire Department working to put out a restaurant fire. This building was once a furniture store and a funeral home owned by Joseph Gorden. It also at one time housed the Salem Encampment No. 84, Independent Order of Odd Fellows, chartered on February 11, 1876. The building standing next to it is the post office in 2009. (Courtesy of Dianna Beaudoin.)

The European Hotel, owned by O. J Hardy, burned down on April 14, 1899. It was located on the corner of Newell and Thirtieth Streets. The fence surrounds the Adam Newell home. Notice the men scrambling to put out the fire. It was not until 1901 that a new hotel was built on this location. (Courtesy of Arthur and Carol DeJongh.)

Hardy rebuilt this hotel in 1901 after a fire. The livery and icehouse stood in back. The hotel was home to many other businesses, including a barbershop, meat market, dance hall, and Post's Ice Cream Parlour. It was struck by lightning and burned again in 1937. Lawrence Jones built his gasoline station on this site. (Courtesy of Stan Navis.)

76

The river was dammed up east of Bunker Hill to run a mill. The road itself was the dam. It stood on the south side of the road, and the pond was on the north side. It froze over in the winter, and the farmers drove their horses and sleighs on the ice. They cut ice and stored it around town in four or five icehouses. Sawdust was packed all around the ice, and it lasted almost until the next winter. It was used to cool the milk at the creamery. Warren Smith remembers his dad putting grain into the boat to take to the mill. As the grain was being ground, he took Warren and his brothers fishing. They caught enough fish to have a tasty meal that night. This photograph was taken around 1900. (Courtesy of Judi Montgomery and Arthur and Carol DeJongh.)

Please provide a caption.

John Schaffer owned this blacksmith and wagon shop. John and Russel Twinning are standing in front of the horses unharnessed from the sleighs. The blacksmith and wagon shop was located in the center of Burnips. One of the sleighs is loaded down with bags of grain; most likely the owner brought them to the mill to be ground. This photograph was taken about 1900. (Courtesy of Arthur and Carol DeJongh.)

Burnips Service Garage was also known as Forest Shuck's blacksmith shop. The gasoline pump out front is an early model with a glass canister on top. The left sign on the front of the building reads Burnips Service Garage. The right-side sign reads the following: "Forest Schuck Horseshoeing, General Repair, Acetylene Welding, Burnips Michigan." (Courtesy of Art Oldenbeck.)

The Covered Wagon Café was owned and operated by Herbert and Eleanor Klinesteker on the corner of Thirtieth and Newell Streets. This restaurant stood between the gasoline station and Teeds Store. The Klinestekers moved it to this location when the oil wells were discovered in 1930s. A second, larger streetcar was placed on this spot in later years. The Klinestekers sold the restaurant to Cleo Feltenbargar around 1940. (Courtesy of Salem Historical Committee.)

Lawrence Jones built this gasoline station in approximately 1938. It was on the corner of Thirtieth and Newell Streets at the same location where the Burnips Hotel stood before it burned down in 1937. Jones and his wife, Dorothy, owned this Phillips 66 gasoline station together for 33 years before they decided to get out of the business. People often came to the station to hang out and catch up on gossip. (Courtesy of Salem Historical Committee.)

Burnips Creamery was built as a wooden structure by Glen Overton in 1892. In 1920, a group of 40 farmers from Salem and Dorr Townships purchased this creamery with notes. In 1936, a new building was constructed in brick. It was sold to a private party in 1948. This building stood on the corner of Thirtieth Street and 143rd Avenue and served as a home for Hudsonville Creamery for many years. (Courtesy of Brent Moomey.)

Local farmers milked their cows each morning, and by afternoon, the milk was delivered to Burnips Creamery. The farmers took turns collecting the milk and taking it to the dairy. Each farmer had initials or markings on their cans. The farmer's wives said if they wanted butter that day, and the driver dropped it off to her. (Courtesy of Crystal Deters.)

Hudsonville Creamery is facing Thirtieth Street in this photograph. In the 1960s, the road was built up, and it now sits above the building, forever changing the landscape. In 1946, Dick Hoezee moved his creamery from Hudsonville to Burnips. The Hoezee family ran this business until 2003, when it was sold to the Landmark Group. The Landmark Group moved it out of Burnips to Holland shortly after. This photograph was taken about 1950. (Courtesy of Lyman and June Moored.)

This 1950s photograph shows Mooreds Implements and dealership. It was owned by Ken and Sadie Moored until their death in a car accident. They sold Oliver farm equipment, repaired tractors, and sold household appliances. The building to the right was the town hall at the time this photograph was taken. These buildings are owned by Oldcastle Glass in 2009. (Courtesy of Lyman and June Moored.)

This early-1900s photograph shows the Adam Newell home and pharmacy. One of the Newell children is standing on the steps of the house. The stools near the door of the store were gave local residents a place to sit and visit. A sign advertising for liver pills, which supposedly cured "sick headache," biliousness, constipation, and bad complexions, is the window of the store. (Courtesy of Arthur and Carol DeJongh.)

This early-1900s photograph shows the Adam Newell home and pharmacy. One of the Newell children is standing on the steps of the house. The stools near the door of the store were a local resting spot for residents to sit and visit. A liver pills sign is in the window of the store. It supposedly cured sick headaches, biliousness, constipation, and bad complexions. (Courtesy of Arthur and Carol DeJongh.)

This store was at one time owned by the Newells, Lipperts, DeJongs, Rynbrandts, and Teed families. The men sitting on the front steps are catching up on the local news. The building just to the right was a tavern run by Ed Drier in the 1930s during the oil days. John Hoeksema bought it and had it torn down. (Courtesy of Bob Teed.)

This unnamed storefront still stands today in 2009 and is known as Teed's Store. Known owners of this store included Luther Perrigo, Adam Newell and his wife, John and Mano Lippert, Marinus and Gertrude Rynbrandt, Nicholas and Ruby DeYoung, and Millard and Hazel Teed. In the early years of this store, it was run as a pharmacy, while other years, it was run as a general store. Millard and Hazel Teed closed the store in 1977. (Courtesy of Stan Navis.)

This Fourth of July photograph from about 1900 shows the community of Salem Township celebrating and gathered around Joseph Gorden's furniture store and undertaking establishment, located in Burnips. All were dressed for this celebration in their Sunday best. The flags proudly blowing in the wind show that these descendents of the early pioneers are thankful to call this home. (Courtesy of Bob Teed.)

Cleo Feltenbarger ran her restaurant during the 1930s. It was a place where locals could come and grab a burger and fries for lunch. The old Allegan County Road Commission Garage stood on the east side of the street. It was built in 1936 by Forest Shuck. It housed the trucks and graders used by the men who worked out of this location. (Courtesy of Lyman and June Moored.)

This photograph from about 1900 depicts Main Street in Burnips Corners looking south. Krieser's Hardware store sits to the right. Notice the signs for equipment on the building, "McCormick" and "Maus San Cultivators." There is a dog standing on the porch steps eagerly awaiting his owner. A little to the south, a horse and buggy is tied to the east side of the road in front of DeJonghs General Store. (Courtesy of Stan Navis.)

This photograph depicts Main Street in Burnips Corners looking north. The building on the immediate right is Joe Gordon's. He was a dealer of school books and stationary, furniture, coffins, and burial robes. He later took a class on embalming and became an undertaker. The upper part of the building was the Independent Order of Odd Fellows lodge. The next building was Sprau's General Store, which was constructed in 1899. The upper part of that building held the Sons of Veterans group. (Courtesy of Stan Navis)

Another photograph of Main Street in Burnips from the 1920s looks south and shows the Hardy Hotel on the right with a Post's Ice Cream Parlour sign in front. The old livery and blacksmith shop on the left, owned by Forest Schuck, indicates the beginning of the automobile era, based on the number of automobiles parked in front. (Courtesy of Margaret Weber.)

Here is a Dibbles social dance handbill, advertising for a dance in Burnips. This hall is believed to have stood on the corner of Thirtieth and 142nd Streets. The Dibble family also owned a general store in Burnips Corners. (Courtesy of Mary Navis.)

Olman Saloon stood in New Salem on the southeast corner of 146th Avenue and Twenty-sixth Street. It was owned and operated by Anton Olman. The building was actually two businesses. One side was the general store, which housed the post office, and the other was a saloon, which only allowed in men. People gathered there to catch up on the local news of the area. Sometime in the early 1900s, it was purchased by Jacob Schumacher, who ran it only a few years before it burned to the ground. This photograph was taken sometime between 1880 and 1903. (Courtesy of Allen Wycoff.)

The old, wooden New Salem store originally housed a blacksmith shop in the rear. A door in the ceiling was used to pull wagons or carriages upstairs for painting. At times, there was a post office in the store. John and George Schichtel, Will Ryan, and Henry Weber Sr. were early proprietors. After the blacksmith was gone, the second floor was used as living quarters. (Courtesy of the Miller family.)

Mercelline Miller stands behind the counter at the New Salem general store in the 1950s. Left of Mercelline is the scale used for weighing bulk products. World War II brought rationing, and some customers had stamps enough to buy only a pound or two. A few pairs of men's work shoes are displayed in front of the counter. Bottles of wine and cigarettes are also in evidence. (Courtesy of the Miller family.)

Alois Schmidt died in 1927 at the age of 29. He had a sliver in his thumb and came down with blood poisoning. They had two flat tires on the way to the hospital. The doctors wanted to amputate his arm, but he would not have it. He left nine children and his wife, Anna, pregnant with twins. This hearse carried him to St. Mary's Cemetery. (Courtesy Shirley Hilaski and Kathleen Cornett.)

Six

CHALKBOARD MEMORIES

Chestock was a one-room schoolhouse known by many names, including District No. 9, Chestog, Chestock, Winchester, and Plainview . The earliest account of this school is from 1879. This is the earliest photograph that has been found. Shown from left to right are (first row) unidentified, Lawrence Kipen, Adam Kipen, unidentified, and Catherine Striegle; (second row) four unidentified, Emma Kipen, Rose Smith, and Elizabeth Kipen; (third row) teacher Mary Moored. It operated as a one-room schoolhouse until 1974. (Courtesy of Margaret Weber and Marian Streb-Albers.)

The little schools all played ball against each other. This was serious business, and all the children practiced hard. The one-room country schoolhouse Chestog defeated the big town school of Burnips. Shown from left to right around 1940 are (first row) Johnny Roe, Rack Roe, and John Brenner; (second row) Margaret Weber and Katie Brenner (third row) Donald Winchester, Robert Weber, and Bill Roe. (Courtesy of Margaret Weber and Marian Streb-Albers.)

Mary Moored was a beloved teacher in Salem Township. She taught in the various one-room schools in this area, including Burnips and Chestog. In the early days, she took her horse and buggy to school, and in later years, her husband, Sherman, drove her to school in their Model T touring car. Moored was still teaching Salem children in her 80s. (Courtesy of Lyman and June Moored.)

The Burnips Corners School was built in 1886 at the cost of $3,000. It stood between Burnips Methodist Church and where the glass factory stands today. The school was sectioned off into two rooms, one held first through fifth grades, and the other held sixth through tenth. The first commencement exercises were held in 1890 for the 10th graders. The building stood until the 1960s, when it was torn down to make room for a new school. (Courtesy of Stan Navis.)

The 10th grade graduates of Burnips High School's class of 1917 are shown. From left to right (first row) Mayme Berens, Beth Goodman, Cora Slagel, Prof. T. T. Gorden, Hattie Sneller, Esther Miller, and Lela Mesick; (second row) Harvey Brandt, George Smith, John Ebmeyer, Marinus VandeBunte, Lambert Geib, John Mellish, and Harry Weaver. (Courtesy of Roberta Becker.)

This 1920 photograph shows Burnips High School's 10th grade class. They were all dressed up in there Sunday best. Some went on to Allegan to attend 11th and 12th grade and possibly go on to the county normal school to become teachers themselves. The only people identified, from left to right, are (first row) Hilda, Laura, Leslie, unidentified, Ethel, and Vesta Loew (Courtesy of Gene and Donna Heasley.)

The 1922 graduating class of Burnips High School proudly poses for this photograph. Shown from left to right are (first row) Lester Simmons, George Phelps, and Margaret Greive (teacher); (second row) Harold Newell, Inez Bailey, Francis Curtis, Beatrice (Johnson) Sheilds, and Marian Smith. (Courtesy of Al Sheilds.)

Students of Burnips School are shown in 1922. From left to right are (first row) Gladys Raab, Lucille Sebright, Grada Fleser, Viola Hildebrand, Muriel Fleser, Frannie Bredeweg, Erma Goodman, and ? Jacobs; (second row) Maurice Smith, Larry Fleser, ? Jacobs, Frankie Kipen, Lyle Bacon, Glen Nynehouse, Esther Sebright, Gertrude Green, and Edna Curtis (second grade); (third row) Bert Cartwright, Gilbert Lippert, Gladys Post, Bernice Bond, Roger Smith, Alger Shuck, Arden Smith, Jim Newell, and unidentified; (fourth row) Marshall Simmons, Lena Sebright, Violet Raab, Roger Cartwright, Florence Goodman, Myrtle Green, Justin Borman, Myrtle Raab, and Martha Fleser; (fifth row) Emberta (Babe) Grooters, Dorothy Bacon, Donna Fleser, Maurice Curtis, and Warren Smith (third grade), Theodore Kipen, and Kenneth Moored; (sixth row) Irene Beck (teacher), Gerald Nynehouse, Louise Sebright, Rosena Kipen, Dorothy Green, Rosena Paffhouse, Evelyn Goodman, and Bertha Fleser. (Courtesy of Susan Welton.)

This 1938 Burnips School photograph shows Boyd Moomey hamming it up in the middle of the front row. Shown from left to right are (first row) Keith Brenner, Francis Brenner, Russ Neinhuis, Dene Smith, Moomey, Robert Zerfaz, Lyman Moored, and Bennie Geib; (second row) Donna Alward, June Moored, Duane Sheib, Max Simmons, unidentified, Calvin Fleser, Howard Jager, Mildred Brenner, and Maxine Simmons; (third row) Cliffard Jager, Francis Shuck, Lester Brower, Doris Raab, Geraldine Sheib, Vonda Levendowski, and Beatrice Denny; (fourth row) Gertude Shuck, Mary Moored (teacher), Crystal Raab, Treasure Moomey, Joyce Yonts, and Majorie Denny. (Courtesy of Lyman and June Moored.)

The students of Burnips School in 1942 are shown. From left to right are (first row) Arlene Stein, Vivian Schieb, Rip Davis, Colleen Parker, Donna Lee Alward, Ethel Goodman, Nelly Ballard, Betty Kamps, and Peggy Sheridan; (second row); Earl Newell, Tom Yost, Ethel Raab, Midge Brenner, Bob Newell; and (third row) ? Pugh, Jim Smith, Howard Jager, ? Trost. (Courtesy of Dene and Colleen Smith.)

Picnics are so much fun, especially with cousins and friends. One can imagine the children chatting back and forth while they sit on a bench with a sandwich or drink in hand. From left to right are Herman Zerfas, Florence Weber, Rose Ann Weber, Dorothy Zerfas, Edman Zerfas, Jerome Weber, Les Weber, and unidentified. (Courtesy of Dorothy Kroll.)

District No. 7 school was also known as the New Salem School. It was mostly attended by the Catholic children from New Salem, and it only went to the 10th grade. The students identified are standing in front a flag with 45 stars in 1914. Shown from left to right are Earl Sutter, Earl, Etta, Catherine, Martha, Isabelle Sutter (teacher), and two unidentified students. (Courtesy of Art Oldenbeck.)

Although no one is named in this 1920s photograph of Maplegrove School, it shows a clear picture of what life was like for these schoolchildren. They are all lined up against the school building eating their lunches out of pails. The toys that they used to entertain themselves are somewhat different from what children use today. The toys that are on the ground in front of the students show that entertainment took imagination and creativity. (Courtesy of Gene and Donna Heasley.)

This is a photgraph from the 1920s of Maplegrove School. From left to right are (first row) Harvey Brower, Orvin Miller, Art Schipper sitting on Jim Browers lap, Leonard Berens, Johnnie Schutter, Marvin Kruithof, unidentified, and Cecil Randt; (second row) Arnold Deters, George Schreur, Garry Berens, Ivan Lezman, Harold Brower, George Engelsman, Bob Freeman, and Gerald Brower; (third row) Gertrude Schutter, Elnora Goodman, Hazel Lezman, Agnes Brower, Raymond "George" Berens, Julia Schipper, Alice Schreur, and Herm Engelsman; (fourth row) Marie Hildebrand, Henrietta Brower, Grace Berens, Frances Berens, Sadie Schipper, Ida Engelsman, Lillian Miller, and Delia Lezman; (fifth row) Harold Van Ommen, George Berens, Tena Engelsman, Gertrude Vanderkolk, Evelyn Deters, Nora Beuge, Henry Engelsman, and teacher Linn Heasley. (Courtesy of Lyle and Betty Browers.)

Franklin School students in 1925 included, from left to right, (first row) Lloyd Hulst, Eselyn Brenner, Melbourne Raab, Gerald Verbeek, Melvin Berens, Earl Berens, Gelmer Winkles, and John Compagner (second row) Alvin South, Ethel Berens, Della Winkles, Jeanette South, Joyce Verbeek, Jean VanderSlik, Muriel Compagner, Ulah Raab, Laura Brenner, and Laura Winkles; (third row) Norwood Buhler, Floyd Brenner, Gerrit Kiekover, Henry Hulst, Russel South, Agnes Raab, Cora VanderSlik, Angeline Van Ommen, Alida VanderSlik, Anna Rynbrandt (teacher), Gladys Compagner, Elnora Raab, Grada VanOmmen, and Arlene Buhler. (Courtesy of Lorne Berens.)

Students at Franklin School are pictured in the fall of 1937. From left to right are (first row) June Vansloten, Ila Harmsen, Lorne Berens, Norma Strickfaden, Jason Boerson, Roger "Chub" Strickfaden, Doug Vansloten, Roger Verbeek, and Clayton Kickover; (second row) Junior Rynbrandt, Laverne Harmsen, Joyce Harmsen, Ester Berens, Marian Winkles, Polly Vansloten, Gorden Verbeek, and Wilmer Timmer; (third row) Vern Berens, Jarvis Boerman, Raymond Winkles, Alan Boersen, Elmer Brenner, Junior Vanderslick, Bernice Timmer, and Florence VanOmmen; (fourth row) Lorne Buhler, Lorna Boerson, Lois Raab, Viola Hildebrand (teacher), Laurene Berens, and Wilma Berens. (Courtesy of Dianna Beaudoin.)

Seven

Furs, Feathers, and Fins

Fred Baachman is standing in front of the barn he built in 1908. One can only surmise that this red-tailed hawk must have been after his chickens. Baachman is proudly displaying the three- to four-foot wingspan of this large bird. Notice the 12 gauge double-barrel shotgun leaning against the barn wall. (Courtesy of Crystal Deters.)

Brothers Fred and Gustaf Baachman are pictured around 1920 after a successful day of hunting. Fred had a farm on 146th Avenue. He enjoyed hunting in his spare time. His brother Gustaf, better known as Doc, was a physician who practiced in Salem. Hanging on the buck pole are two eight-point bucks and a doe. (Courtesy of Dorothy Paffhouse.)

Clyde and Warren Smith show off their catch in 1935. The brothers are holding their catch of pheasants and rabbits. Wearing the feathers in their hats was the thing to do during this time. They hunted in Burnips, Mudlake, and sometimes Dorr. The men dressed their catch, and their mother, Elizabeth, cooked it for the family to enjoy. (Courtesy of Shirley Schepers.)

In this 1940s photograph, Burnips residents Elmer Smith and his son Dene are holding up their catch of bluegill caught at East Lake near Hopkins, using a rented wooden boat on a miserable rainy day. Dene and his mother, Elizabeth (Lizzie), cleaned the fish when they got home and enjoyed a good supper. (Courtesy of Shirley Schepers)

Warren Smith, recently back from the service, spent the day fishing with his father Elmer. Here they proudly display their catch of bluegills caught that day on Bellagraph Lake near Hopkins. They often fished together when they could and had a fish fry with family and friends. (Courtesy of Warren Smith.)

In this 1942 photograph, brothers Oscar and Dean Smith are standing in their front yard on 143rd Avenue in Burnips, proudly holding up the 42-inch pike they caught down by the hogback. The hogback was a local fishing hole near the Rabbit River just south of Burnips near George Simmon's home. A comedian, Dean is displaying his gun as if he just shot the fish. (Courtesy of Shirley Schepers.)

One day, as friends George Schneider and John Miller sat visiting, they planned a fishing trip together. The men hunted and fished together on a regular basis. They enjoyed telling tall tales and fish stories. They sat in their boat with poles in hand, waiting for a bite. This day, they caught their limit. (Courtesy of the Miller family.)

Oker Gorden was born and raised in Salem. Later in life he moved to Grand Rapids but came home often to hunt with his friend Morton Wells. The two are shown with the squirrels of today's hunt. Gordon's folks, William and Martha, who lived just north of Burnips on Thirtieth Street, sent him home with the fruits and vegetables they raised. (Courtesy of Art Oldenbeck.)

Duck hunting was a sport, but it also meant dinner for the family. Anything caught in the field or stream was used on the dinner table to supplement what the farm produced. This day, four friends got together to hunt, and it looks it was a success. Pictured from left to right are Art Rewa, Raymond Weber, Jack Rewa, and Pearl Johnson. (Courtesy of Dorothy Kroll.)

This photograph is of Bob Teed holding on to his new dog and his gun. All laid out in front of him are the four pheasants and rabbit he shot that day. Teed's parents owned Teeds Store in Burnips. As a young man, he was often seen helping out in the store. (Courtesy of Sheila Buckleitner.)

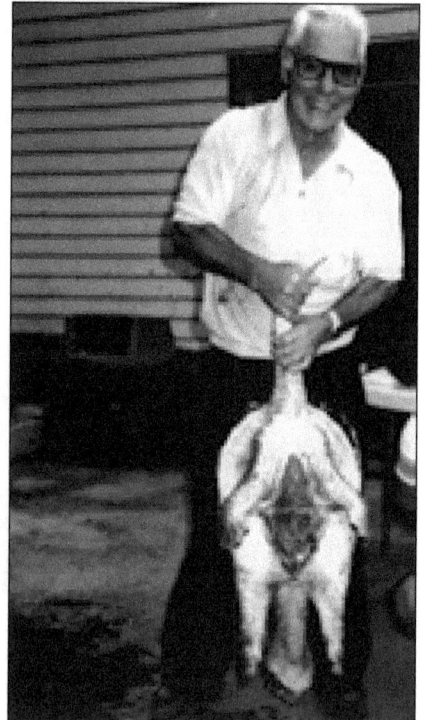

This photograph shows John Pitsch, a Burnips resident who was known for the snapping turtles he caught. This was one of the bigger ones. Pitsch and his wife, Francis, were the parents of 11 children, all of whom grew up in Burnips. He also raised his youngest brother Ronald after their parents died. Pitsch was known as the original scrap recycler. His son James is the township supervisor in 2009. (Courtesy of the Pitsch family.)

Eight

FUN WITH FAMILY AND FRIENDS

Watching local baseball teams was a beloved pastime for many who lived in Salem. This photograph shows the Salem baseball team in the early 1900s. Shown from left to right are (first row) John DeJongh, Elmer Smith, and Harvey Miller; (second row) Bill Fleser, Art DeJongh, and Fred Miller; (third row) Claude Gibson, Glenn Sebrights, Jake Fleser, and Fred Strugis. (Courtesy of Brent Moomey.)

This 1930 photograph shows the Burnips High School basketball team. From left to right are (first row) Harry Fleser, Clarence Paffhouse, James Newell (holding the basketball) and Charles Cartwright; (second row) Ken Moored, Harold Vanomen, Paul Brower (teacher), and Norward Buhler. These young, skinny men played various teams in the area. (Courtesy of Shirley Schepers.)

Sweethearts Oliver Perry and Jella (Moore) Moored are out for a Sunday drive. They are enjoying a ride in their horse-drawn buggy through Burnips Corners. Jella is all fancied up in her Sunday dress and new flowered hat. They lived north of Burnips on Thirtieth Street on section nine. They were married on September 27, 1888, in Osecola Township. (Courtesy of Lyman and June Moored.)

These Burnips men are enjoying refreshments after a ball game. Shown from left to right are (first row) Clarence "Doc" Paffhouse and Harry Brenner; (second row) Merle Payne, Keith Hyde, Alvin Boerman, and Gerald Yonker. One can see by the look on their faces that they probably won the game. It looks like they are having a lot of fun. (Courtesy of Dorothy Paffhouse.)

The authors could not resist including this to show that no matter how hard life was, there was always a time to enjoy each other's company. Some of the people pictured are Daniel and Julia Brenner, with their sons Dan and Walter. Daniel and Julia settled in Salem Township in 1868. (Courtesy of Dorothy Paffhouse.)

Salem lodge No. 169, of the Independent Order of Odd Fellows was chartered on August 24, 1871, at Burnips Corners. The Odd Fellows hall was completed and dedicated by the lodge on August 24, 1874. Those identified in this photograph are Joseph Goodman, Joseph Gorden, William Miller, David Goodman, Frederick Sutter, Christian Sutter, ? Sprau, George Heck, and William Gorden. (Courtesy of Brent Moomey.)

Local farmers were asked to help build the sandy trails into roadbeds. After completing their own chores, they took their teams of horses to the sand-filled roads to roll the gravel onto the roadbeds. The roadbed they are working on was at 143rd Avenue just east of Burnips. The only men identified in this photograph are Pearl Goodman and Peter Selby. (Courtesy of Roberta Becker.)

William A. and Sarah (Willyard) Curtis took their children to visit her parents, Milo Clyde and Lena (Brower) Willyard. Sarah had brothers in the military. Shown from left to right are (first row) Maurice and Edna; (second row) Sarah and baby Lauren Curtis wrapped in a flag, unidentified, cousin Kit, William A., Lena, and Milo Clyde. This photograph was taken around 1916. (Courtesy of Susan Welton.)

There was always time for fun even with the busy life of a farmer. Here Lambert Schipper, dressed as a woman, and Edward Hulst, dressed as a man, are having some of that fun. They were good friends and neighbors and loved clowning around. Times did not have to feel so hard when there was humor. What a stylish bonnet on Schipper's head. (Courtesy of Lyle and Betty Brower.)

Forrest Shuck and his two friends are getting ready to visit relatives in Ohio. They brought two extra tires because the ones on their car were so bad that they would not make it. This 1912 Model T touring car could travel about 35 to 40 miles an hour. It was a long trip for these three, but by today's standards, it would only take a few hours. (Courtesy of Art Oldenbeck.)

The Sons of Union Veterans Civil War camps were named after a fallen or a decorated soldier. This band was named after Godliep Miller, a Salem Township man who was captured and died in Andersonville Prison. The building they are standing in front of was just east of the mill on 142nd Avenue. This photograph was taken around 1900. (Courtesy of Art Oldenbeck.)

Show in this photograph are friends Ivan Lippert and Clyde Smith standing on the corner of Thirtieth Street and 142nd Avenue. They looked like a couple of vagabonds, wearing hats that were common for the time of this mid-1920s photograph. Lippert's father, Jack, owned Lipperts Grocery in Burnips. (Courtesy of Warren Smith.)

Five friends, pictured from left to right in the 1920s, are Elmer Smith, unidentified, Joe Fleser, and two unidentified. These jokesters were in a Model T Ford, showing that Prohibition was not strictly enforced in Salem Township. Although it is not known if there really was alcohol in these bottles, they are having fun and are clearly showing their disregard for the law. (Courtesy of Warren Smith.)

Which way is home? This unidentified girl is standing at the Bunker Hill crossroads of 142nd Avenue and Thirtieth Street. The road to Dorr is at her back, while she is pointing towards Burnips. It appears that the mill pond is still present. The landscape changed drastically when the mill pond was drained and the road paved. (Courtesy of Warren Smith.)

Living on the farm meant lots of chores but also pets. This photograph was taken on the Curtis farm, just east of Bunker Hill. Clyde Curtis enjoyed his pets, as he is shown with his pet rabbit on his head. Shown from left to right are (first row) Maurice, Kenneth Willyard, Edna, Lauren, Clara, and Homer Lewis; (second row) Clyde, Francis, and Viola holding her sister Lena. (Courtesy of Susan Welton.)

Friends and cousins gathered to admire Jim Dargie's 1920s Ford Model T touring car. There were still horses and buggies being used at this time, and a new automobile was cause for excitement. The group had their photo taken with the Model T. Shown from left to right are (first row) Henry Wycoff, Harry Wycoff, and Lilton Wycoff; (second row) Darga, Peter Kipen, and Cyrus Dusendang. (Courtesy of Susan Welton.)

Farming is hard work. Taking the time to find one's inner child brightens a person's day. Milo Clyde Willyard is taking a break from his daily chores to swing a while. Granddaughter Edna Kipen remembered him as liking to laugh and joke with her. He was born around 1863. His wife, Lena, and he lived in the Diamond Springs area. (Courtesy of Susan Welton.)

Here is the William Wies family showing off their first automobile, a 1914 Model T, to their family. From left to right are Amelia (Emma) Fleser, Katherine (Katie) (Fleser) Weis, Elizabeth (Fleser) Strickfaden, William Wies, mother Christina Fleser, and Grace and William Fleser with baby Harry in Grace's arms and barefooted Donald and Faith. (Courtesy of Lorne Berens.)

Close only counts in horseshoes, as brothers-in-law, David Brenner, Lloyd Moomey, and Jacob Hildbrand are finding. They are enjoying a game of horseshoes together. The sound of the horseshoe clanged if they hit the mark. A lot of time was spent enjoying the camaraderie. This was a common form of entertainment played in Salem Township. (Courtesy of Roberta Becker.)

Donna Loew turned six years old in 1910. Here she is surrounded by friends and family at her birthday party. All were dressed in their Sunday best with bows in their hair to attend the party. Donna is the little girl standing behind the chocolate cake. She was the daughter of Martin and Lottie Loew, and they lived on Thirty-second Street between 144th and 146th Avenues. (Courtesy of James Beyer.)

Young Jacob Steffes lived near the New Salem area on Twenty-fifth Street. He is shown here with a solemn expression, posing with his accordion-like squeeze box. He is all dressed up in his Sunday best for this photograph. Steffes was well known for his ability to play the squeeze box. (Courtesy of Al Wycoff.)

These three New Salem friends are posing for a photograph, holding their musical stringed instruments. Shown from left to right are John Weber, John Funk, and Jim Dargie. The trio enjoyed getting together and playing for their own enjoyment. Weber and Dargie played the fiddle, while Funk played the cello. (Courtesy of Al Wycoff.)

Weber had recently purchased this 1913 REO and wanted a picture taken of it. He was an avid photographer. He also owned the store that the car was parked in front of. He had the four men jump in the car with wrapped cigars from the store, which were returned to the shelf after the photograph was taken. From left to right are Fred Weist, J. P. Schumaker, Henry Weber, and Anthony Schumaker. The photograph is from about 1914. (Photograph by John Weber; courtesy of Al Wycoff.)

Nine

THOSE WHO SERVED THE COUNTRY

Dene Smith is being comical in this 1952 photograph, posing with a dead pheasant and pretending to feed it. Smith and his partner Eddie Anderson were stationed in Korea at this water purifying station. They were hungry for fresh meat when Smith saw this pheasant wandering around in the fields and decided to go after it. Smith said although it tasted good, it was pretty tough. (Courtesy of Dene and Colleen Smith.)

Seventeen-year-old Boyd Moomey is pictured at Great Lakes Naval Training Station in April 1942. He served from March 25, 1942, to January 31, 1946. During his tour of duty, he was a radioman and a gunner on the USS *Saratoga*. Later while serving on the USS *Manilla Bay* aircraft carrier, he was on board a TBM. He survived a crash in the Pacific Ocean southwest of the Hawaiian Islands. (Courtesy of Brent Moomey.)

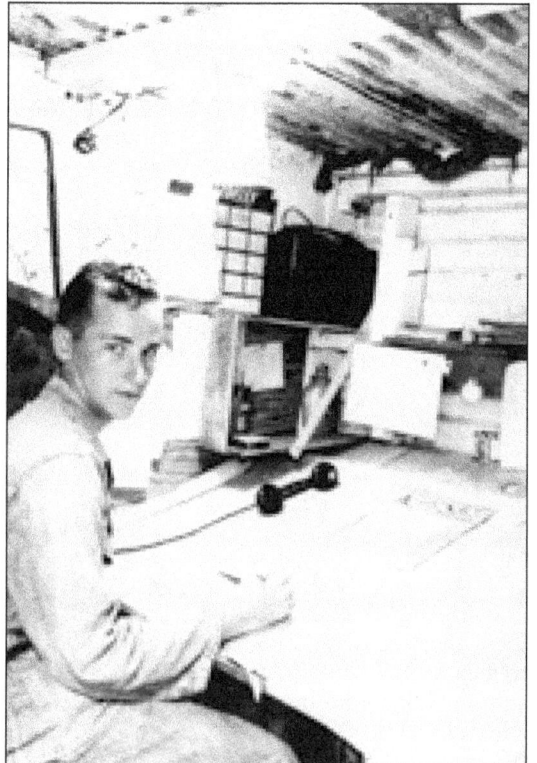

Arden "Speed" Smith is sitting at his desk while on watch. Years later, he told his granddaughter that in order to take this photograph of himself, he tied a string from his foot to the camera to snap the picture. Smith served in the army with the 105th Field Artillery Battalion, 27th Division. They supported advancing American Marines and infantry in Okinawa. (Courtesy of Warren Smith.)

Sgt. Clarence Deters was stationed near Nuremburg, Germany, in 1945. He was 22 years old when he was inducted into the U.S. Army Air Corps in August 1941. He married Crystal Loew in Greensboro, South Carolina, on February 21, 1945, and two days later, he was sent to Europe (England, France, and Germany). He returned home after his discharge and started a plumbing and heating business. (Courtesy of Crystal Deters.)

Deters is standing in the window handing a paper to Sergeant Gallaway. Lieutenant Olsen is standing in the doorway of a field office on April 24, 1945. This field office appears to have been a German railroad car at one time. The automobile on the side seems to be a general's car. Deters was in the 425th NFS of the U.S. Army Air Force. (Courtesy of Crystal Deters.)

This photograph of Chris Strickfaden was taken in front of his sister Elizabeth Smith's home in Burnips on July 4, 1918. Strickfaden was dressed in his military uniform but was hamming it up by holding an old army musket he had found at his sister's house. He served in World War I, where he was wounded by shrapnel. (Courtesy of Loren and Vivian Buhler.)

Leo Funk was a private during World War I. He served with barracks No. 0474. While in the service, he received the Great War for Civilization medal. On it were the countries France, Italy, Serbia, Japan, Montego, Russia, CRFFC, Great Britain, Belgium, Brazil, Portugal, Rumania, and China. Funk delivered mail as part of his tour of duty while serving in the Philippines. He was a lifelong resident of Burnips. (Courtesy of Elaine Kimber.)

120

George Goodman, son of David and Jennie Goodman, is shown here around 1918 practicing maneuvers for a tour of duty in World War I. Using a bayonet, he is honing his hand-to-hand combat skills with this makeshift dummy made of sticks. He returned home to Salem Township without any injuries or scars from serving his country. (Courtesy of Roberta Becker.)

"I'm home on leave" are words every family member loved to hear. Pictured here is Luther Hildebrand home on leave, spending time with his sweetheart Dee Alward and his parents, Jacob and Beth Hildebrand. Their time together was precious, as he was getting ready to go back, and they did not know when they would see him again. Luther served in World War II. (Courtesy of Roberta Becker.)

The Smith family made the trip to Fort Sill, Oklahoma, to see their son Arden on December 30, 1941. He was shipped overseas and served in the Pacific theater. Shown from left to right are Elizabeth Smith (mother), Arden, Elmer Smith (father), Warren Smith, and Gale Smith. They were allowed one hour to visit, and no passes were allowed. Elizabeth's emotions were written on her face. Arden was discharged in October 1945. (Courtesy of Shirley Schepers.)

Sometime during World War I Adeline (Schmidt) Striegle and her brother Ed Schmidt were visiting their mother when this photograph was taken. She married Joseph Striegle in 1936 and farmed just north of Plainview School. Schmidt drove a medical truck until he received shrapnel to his legs. He then worked in the hospital. (Courtesy of Shirley Hilaski.)

Ten

OIL DAYS

This 1930s photograph is of six unidentified men sitting on an oil rig, getting ready to start a full days work. Each man had a specific job to do. Men came from all over the state to work in the oil fields. These men are enjoying a lighthearted moment, clowning around for the camera. This oil rig was identified as number five, located in the New Salem area. (Courtesy David Weber.)

Salem Township was fortunate to have oil and natural gas found within the township. These roughnecks were covered in oil, as it gushed from the well on Sutter number one. The photograph was shot in February 1938 on the Fred Sutter farm. The only person identified is Leonard Kraft, standing in the back. (Courtesy of Art Oldenbeck.)

This 1938 photograph shows the roughnecks working on Sutter number one. The Muskegon-based oil company subleased this land from the Gorden Wilson Company, who had leased it from Fred Sutter. The only person identified in this photograph is Leonard Craft on the left. The roughnecks are covered with oil from the when the well blew. (Courtesy of Art Oldenbeck.)

This 1930s photograph of Chapman number one shows an unidentified man holding on to a shut-off value. After the well was capped, a shut-off value was put in place to control the flow of oil. Although the area looks chaotic with bits, chains, pipes, and boards, the oil workers knew where every piece of equipment was. (Courtesy of David Weber.)

This 1930s photograph of well number five shows a lone man standing on the station. Although he was not one of the workers, he had come to visit. The steel cable was wrapped around the wooden draw works and attached to the hardened bit. The hardened bit beat through layers of rock and soil. (Courtesy of David Weber.)

Oil well number five is spewing oil or mud above the station. The pipe that was driven down the well is all laid out in front, waiting for another section to be driven down the hole. The pipe was pulled into position by a steel cable, which was then driven into the well. The two men are unidentified in this 1930s photograph. (Courtesy of Dave Weber.)

This photograph shows the oil gushing from the hole the men had worked so hard to drill. The explosion comes from hitting pockets of gas as the pipes are pounded into the earth. The oil workers never knew when the explosion would gush out. There were times that beautiful, black oil would blow, or it could be just mud and water. (Courtesy of Dave Weber.)

This pump jack, also called a horse head, is still present in Salem Township in 2009 in many areas. The jack pumped the oil into the pipes that are shown in the front. The oil then was pumped into storage tanks, and tanker trucks came in and hauled the oil away. (Courtesy of Dave Weber.)

These three unidentified men are leaning up against the shack also known as the dog house. These buildings were hastily constructed to house the large engines used to drive the oil equipment. The men's clothes are covered in oil and dirt after their long day in the oil fields. The photograph was taken in the 1930s. (Courtesy of Dave Weber.)

Visit us at
arcadiapublishing.com